ART GLASS
Breaking Glass To Make Money

A   BEGINNERS GUIDE TO
MAKING MONEY WITH   ART GLASS
COPPER FOIL AND LEAD WORK EXPLAINED

~ Francis Elder II

ART GLASS - BREAKING GLASS TO MAKE MONEY

A Beginners Guide To Making Money With Art Glass Copper Foil And Lead Work Explained

---

© Francis Elder II - Creations By Elder
PO Box 782   Kansas, OK 74347
frank@creationsbyelder.com

1st Edition August 2016

www.creationsbyelder.com

This work may not be reproduced, copied or re-distributed in any form or fashion without the written consent of the author.

Introduction

My name is Francis Elder II and my voyage into stained glass began back in 1988 while I was still in high school in Siloam Springs, Arkansas. I always liked to take art and you could find me doodling on a piece of scrap paper at any given moment in time.

Our shop trades teacher Louie knew this and asked me if I would like to help with a project he wanted to do for V.I.C.A. (Vocational Industrial Clubs of America), which turned out to be a set of three stained glass panels. I thought this would be a lot of fun and said yes.

From there I helped with the drawing of the design, then the full sized pattern and then contributed my time to help actually produce the panels. A wonderful lady by the name of Beatrice Stebbing who owned a stained glass studio in town donated her expertise, time and materials to help accomplish this project. She was one of the kindest and most inspiring people I had met

I guess she must have seen something in me because she called me up out of the clear blue one day and asked me to come to work for her. So while still in high school I started on my path to learning this wonderful art. In the years since I have worked for other studios as well as operating my own studio.

I consider myself an average, ordinary guy that is just trying to follow his dream and provide for his family by doing something that he loves. Somehow I have been given this gift and ability to "visualize" and create. As most other artist's will tell you, I am my own worst critic.

I am lucky to have one of my children that has taken a very keen interest in learning this art / trade and I am teaching him all that I know in the hopes that he will continue forward and be able to one day pass this knowledge on to others himself.

My goal with this book is to not only help inspire you to follow your dreams of working with art glass but also see that there are ways to make money in doing so. Passing along this knowledge to you is my attempt to help keep this art / trade vibrant and healthy.

The only way manufacturers and wholesalers stay in business is if there is sufficient demand for the products that they sell. "Mom and Pop" type shops are what this country is built on and how communities flourish. I hope you find this information useful and inspiring.

Table of Contents

Introduction	i

CHAPTER 1

Do What You Love	1
You Are Part of Your Art	2
Customer Satisfaction	3

CHAPTER 2

Designs - The Basics	4, 5
Keeping it Simple	6
Designing Made Easier	7
Choosing Designs to Make Money	8, 9
Pattern Making And Storage	10, 11

CHAPTER 3

Efficiency For The Win	12
Pattern Pieces Or No Pattern Pieces	13
Size Does Matter	14
Make Those Scraps Count	15

CHAPTER 4

Production	16
Multiples Versus One At A Time	17
Custom Orders	18
Materials	19, 20

CHAPTER 5

Safety	21
Getting The Lead Out	22
Glass Can Bite!	23
Warnings And Lead Disclosures	24
Wear Goggles At All Times	25

CHAPTER 6

Selling Price And Charges	26
Learn Your Market	27
Quality Matters	28
Formula For Success	29, 30, 31
Installation And Service Calls	32, 33

CHAPTER 7

Where And How To Sell	34
Must Haves	35, 36, 37
Other Helpful Items To Get	38
Insurance	39
Farmers Markets	40
Craft Fairs And Selling Events	41
Flea Markets	42, 43
Galleries And Commission Sales	44, 45
Social Media	46
In Summary	47

CHAPTER 8

Make It To Last	48
Proper Construction Method	49
Reinforcement	50

CHAPTER 9

Marketing	51
Cards And Fliers	52
Banners	53
Farmers Markets	54
Coupons	55, 56
Contact Logs	57
Signing Your Work	58, 59
Social Media	60
Track Your Efforts	61

CHAPTER 10

Donations And Family	62
Donations	63, 64
Family	65

CHAPTER 11

Teaching	66
Cross Training	67, 68
In Summary	69

CHAPTER 12

Going Forward	70

Do What You Love

Find and focus on what brings you happiness and when you can do that in your professional life you will wake up each morning with a sense of purpose to drive you through the day!

So many times in our lives we are stuck in jobs and professions that we feel "sap our souls", or so the saying goes.

I am here to tell you that does not need to be the case. You obviously have a love for working with glass and if you have bought this book it is because you feel there is more to your work than it just being a "hobby".

Don't get me wrong, there is nothing wrong with doing art / stained glass work as a hobby and I have seen folks that consider themselves "hobbyists" that execute technique and have an understanding of this type of work that rivals many "professional" studios.

There is a big difference from doing this as a hobby though and doing it for profit to pay your bills, put food on your table and so on. And that difference really is in your mind first and foremost. You have to "flip a switch" in a way and start thinking a little bit differently.

I have heard folks talk about how they would never want to take something they love and try to make a living at that, because then they feel it would become work and would kill the pleasure of what it is that they do. And that is silly. You determine if you stay in a good mindset or not.

Just remember that it takes a lot of hard work to get something good to happen, but just because it is hard work doesn't mean it has to lose the "fun".

You Are Part Of Your Art

Many times when glass artists refer to putting "themselves" into their art, they love to refer to that as blood, sweat and tears. Sometimes that is almost literal.

There is more to it than that saying though. Each of us has our own distinct styles, talents, likes and dislikes.

There is nothing stopping you from expressing things you love in your work and in fact that is part of what will set you apart from others.

For me, I love to create kaleidoscopes because I like my art to be interactive and to beckon the viewer of the item to become more than just a static observer and more of an interactive observer.

So I create everything from the regular three sided glass scopes all the way to incorporating them into free standing sculptural pieces. I love to embellish them with decorative soldering and do things with them that make them unique, which is why I normally sell my scopes for a couple of hundred dollars apiece on the low end and to just around a thousand dollars apiece on the high end.

Maybe you like to fish or have other hobbies you really enjoy. There is nothing stopping you from doing pieces that are related to hobbies you like, as long as there is a market, go for it.

Now with that said, it is easy to create pieces that you look at and say "I would buy that" and then wonder why folks aren't just swooping in and buying them up. You have to cater to your market and I will get deeper into that further in to the book.

Customer Satisfaction

Are customers right 100% of the time? No. That is the short answer.

The long answer is, well, a bit longer.

From this point forward you have to remember that your customers are your lifeblood. Keeping them satisfied is paramount and job number one.

Many people equate keeping their prices down as low as possible to being the key factor in keeping their customers happy. That is not true. And not only is it not true, but it is a determinate to doing business and the longevity of your business.

There will be times that you just have to "grin and bear it" while dealing with tough customers, but remember that they can help you succeed. And if you think of them as a partner to your success it makes it much easier to deal with those few that will be a bit harder to deal with than most. And you never know when that one client that is very demanding might suddenly spend enough with you to take care of your bills for a month or two.

Follow up is key to your customer satisfaction. If you tell someone you are going to get back to them by a certain date with a quote, other information, finished product etc... then you had better do so. And follow up is also key to generating new work, I will get into that also later in the book.

When the customer is being treated with respect and feel that they are the king or queen, they will come back to you over and over again.

If a customer is wrong about something, there is almost always going to be a way to deal with the situation that will not offend them. Many times it comes down to educating your customer so that they can better understand what is going on.

Designs - The Basics

We all have within us the ability to create and draw from our imagination the spark of creation. Open your mind and your soul and you too will find your own spark!

There are a number of areas I want to touch on in regards to this subject as well as touch base on my understanding of some of the legalese of the subject too.

First of all, designing from scratch really is not as hard as you may think and I am going to talk to you about ways to help you do that for small to large projects. I plan on authoring several in depth how-to books in the future for technique and such, but for now I want to give you a basic understanding of the subject.

First and foremost in regards to copyright I have this to say. Just because you see it online, posted to a social media site, in a book or so on, doesn't mean that the author/artist of the work has given you permission to copy the piece, for profit or not for profit.

Just because you are recreating something to give-a-way does not keep you from violating copyright laws. Now with that said, I am not a copyright expert. Certain things I have learned from my own trial and error as well as doing research on my own. If you have questions, do some research on your own or get advice from an actual copyright attorney.

There are lots of patterns available that have special use permissions. A good example are the Spectrum Pattern of the Month collection. They allow for individual use, but beyond that Spectrum Glass informs you to contact the original artist/designer to get permission from them directly.

Also, various pattern books will have the same type of restrictions while others will allow any and all duplication to be done of their works. Read the books carefully, they will tell you. Just remember you are now stepping into something a bit different, where you will be putting a public face to your work.

And lets not forget licensing for things such as sports club logos, university mascots and such.

These are items that people love to reproduce but when you are a business and making money on selling items you had better have your ducks in a row. If you want to reproduce a college, university, team logo you have to get permission and generally speaking a license.

Those licenses will usually consist of an application fee that is non-refundable. The application process can be a pain and pretty extensive but if you really want to reproduce those kinds of items, this is the process you are going to have to follow.

Then they generally get a percentage of the sale. There could also be other stipulations.

Me personally, I have found that it just does not warrant the amount spent, because you normally have to renew your license each year as well.

Keeping It Simple

Now that you are on your voyage to becoming paid for the work that you do, you have to consider several different aspects and one of those is design.

I think most of us would like to just work on unique and one of a kind pieces all day long, I know I would. But the fact of the matter is that unless you are established and have built a good clientele, you are going to be doing lots of "smalls" to help pay the bills.

I have developed lots of designs for sun catchers that work around holidays, seasons, what is the "in" thing currently and so on.

In addition, I have made these patterns so that they are easily duplicated. So that I can sit down and make a half a dozen, dozen or more at a time. Time. That is the key word here. Time is money.

You will want to develop a dozen or more patterns that are easily made. For instance, one of the "in things" for decorating right now are owls. I have a specific pattern for a cute little hoot owl that I turn around and sell for $9 each. Doesn't sound like much does it?

Well, I can create about 7 of these per hour. And this is factoring in the total time to cut, grind, foil, solder, patina etc...

That works out to $63 per hour of product made, before taking away for cost of materials. By the time all the costs to produce and sell are figured in, it is still a pretty darn good amount per hour I make on these little guys.

You will want to have items that are in that $10 to $15 range if possible. You do not need a lot of them, but 3 or 4 items in that price range appeals to those that are looking for "economical" gifts. And then they will start spending more money with you down the road.

I have found that items in the price range of $15 to $25 are the ones that sell most often on average.

Designing Made Easier

There is a lot of new technology that can help with designing patterns. I use software developed by a well known graphics company and there are also several pieces of software out there that are specific to the art / stained glass industry. If you would like information about the specific software that I use please contact me.

There are several "old school" ways to help you create your own designs.

With so many patterns and pattern books out there it is easy to take inspiration from several and combine "aspects" from each to create your own pattern. Again, I am not saying to violate any copyright laws, but there is nothing stopping you from taking inspiration from patterns and books that are out there and redoing it into something that is unique to yourself. You can't just reproduce a pattern in whole into a larger pattern that has other design elements, you have to "tweak" it to make it your own.

In addition, you can use photos to help create patterns.

For instance, lets say you wanted to create a hummingbird pattern from scratch. After some searching you have come across a photo of a hummingbird, not of a pattern or a drawing, but a photo of an actual hummingbird.

You print it out and then you can take a sharpie marker and "outline" all the main areas. The body, the wings, the tail, the beak and so on. Then you take a piece of blank paper and lay over that other one. I have a video on my YouTube channel about this.

Hopefully you have a light table, but if not you can use a window in your house. You can then trace over the original you printed out and create a nice little black and white. From there you add in your break lines. Keep a binder with your originals in it and always work from copies.

Now you have a pattern for a suncatcher. And in addition to that, you now have a design element for a larger piece. So if someone wants to have a small window made with a humming bird in it, you have the humming bird. All you have to do is draw out the perimeter of the panel, add in a border if needed/wanted, place the humming bird in it by tracing it in, maybe add a flower the same way you did with the hummingbird, add in break lines and viola', you have a full sized pattern for a window.

Enlarging or reducing the suncatcher pattern is easy. Today you can purchase a printer/scanner very cheaply that also reduces or enlarges what it is copying. Spending less than a hundred dollars will really help you in the long run.

Choosing Designs to Make Money

First you have to determine several designs to make that will appeal to your market. Are you going to do craft shows that appeal to a broad base of customers? Are you going to do specialty shows, such as sci-fi, Meta-Physical, etc..?

For me I have numerous designs that carry over to a large audience, I place importance on having a diverse selection of offerings.

To give you an example, some of the suncatchers I have are; crosses, owls, southwestern, automobile, birds, flowers, whimsical, cats, dogs, mice, Egyptian, spiders, cancer ribbons, peace signs, Christmas trees, pumpkins, angels, peace signs, yin yang symbols, just to name a few. Then I have other items like candle holders, sculptural type pieces, kaleidoscopes, desk art, and more.

Then I have several larger panels that will range in price of $200 to just under $300. I have more of the $200 to $300 panels, versus say for instance only one panel that is right at $3000. That higher end piece draws folks in as a "wow" piece.

For my suncatchers I probably sell more of the $10 to $25 ones cumulatively than the larger panels. But the larger panels show folks what I am capable of and help generate custom orders.

You will want to come up with some simple designs that you can duplicate easily and efficiently. Take for instance a cross. It is a simple design and one that people buy a lot of from me. I have a small cross that is about 3" wide by 5" tall. They are simple to make and I can even use up a lot of my scrap.

You can cut your scrap up into strips with a system of tools that plug into plastic grid works, this grid system has plug in guides to cut repetitive geometric shapes quickly and accurately.

I will pick out scraps or small sheets and cut up the strips I want, and then set it up to cut those strips into the two or three or four different lengths. I can spend a couple of hours and knock out enough glass to make 2 or 3 dozen crosses.

Now with the crosses being pretty much straight lines, there is not much need for grinding if any at all. But if you do need to grind, set them all off to the side and wait and do it at once. Remember, efficiency in time is what will make you more money for the effort you put into this.

Then after cutting and grinding you sit down and foil them all up. After which you tin all the pieces and move on to assembly.

All the time you are doing this you are studying the way you work and thinking about ways you can shave off time in your production. Ways you can be faster while still giving a good product. This comes with time and experience. But as long as you are keeping in the back of your mind that you want to be more efficient then you will become more efficient. And that in turn will lead to greater profits.

In the afore mentioned example of the small cross suncatchers the profit really comes from being able to produce many at once. I produce 2 to 3 dozen at a time, because I know they will sell. I would not produce that quantity though of other items at one time, but instead maybe 1/2 a dozen to a dozen instead.

I can produce approximately 8 of those crosses per hour. I sell them for $10 each. My cost for materials is negligible, but lets say it costs me 50 cents each in material, that is foil, solder, flux. Then lets say it works out to where I am spending $1 each for electricity, food, water. All this is assuming I am working at home and have no lease/rent for a studio, but I still need to factor in a portion of my regular bills to really try and have an accurate cost to produce the item.

Plugging in those kinds of numbers I am now at somewhere around $68 per hour for making those little crosses.

Then of course there are the costs for transportation, entry fees for selling events, etc...

If you really start looking at this as your "business" you will make better decisions in regards to design, pricing and overall offerings of products.

Pattern Making and Storage

You can use various materials that stand the test of time better than others, in regards to your pattern making. But first and foremost you have to get into the mindset that these patterns you create have value. A lot of value.

What that means is that you need to preserve your originals in such a way that they can be duplicated, months, years or decades down the road. I like to store mine in poster mailing tubes, normally rolled up with rubber bands holding them closed. I do not like to fold them because the crease can cause inaccuracy when it is being folded out. And I do not like to make the rolls as tight as possible.

Once you get a lot of designs you will want to look at some alternate ways of doing your storage, such as lateral shelves or hanging vertically.

Now we come back to that little thing called Copyright. Once you have created an original design, it is yours. You do not have to "file" for a copyright, those provisions and protections are granted to you automatically. If you have to sue someone, well that might be a good time to get your copyright on the design.

You have to show providence to the design, and that you actually own it. This means dating and signing your art, taking photos etc... Anything that can prove in a court of law that you are the original designer/artist for that pattern.

Personally, when I have someone ask me if they can copy a pattern I have created, I tell them no. The reason I do that is because I have worked hard to create these patterns and designs and each one represents money in the form of unique product to make and sell.

Now with that said, there is nothing stopping you from selling your patterns, make some money from them if you can. At a dollar a copy for a suncatcher pattern, why not? You might charge $5 to $20 per full sized pattern or even publish a book of patterns.

You can also attach specific "license" terms, where they can not be used for commercial use etc...

For designs that I am only going to make one of, I normally just work off of the original art. I will not create a "cartoon" (duplicate) as that adds a lot of time to the process. I actually use a light table, put down my pattern and then score the glass, providing I can see the pattern through the glass. Many times I have used a new sharpie and "blacked out" the lines so that they are seen better through the glass. If I have to make a cartoon for one or two pieces I do, I just stick a piece of paper over the pattern for that piece, copy it, cut it out, place it on the glass, mark around it, and then score it.

The reason I tend to do the above is because of efficiency. When you are doing glass work for money, being in the red or the black is many times a result of how efficient you are in what you do.

If I am able to cut my production time down by say 20% that means I am making more money on that project. That also means I have more time to work on other projects, which again makes me more money.

For patterns that you are going to repeat a lot there are several ways to create the cartoon pieces you will use to duplicate the piece. Thick brown paper stock, think of the old fashioned grocery bags, works nicely. As does Vellum, modern "paper vellum" aka vegetable vellum is used for a variety of purposes including plans, technical drawings and blueprints.

You could also use plastic sheeting. Just be careful, when you transfer the pattern to this type of sheeting it is easy to "smear" the lines.

I have developed a technique where I use glass to create my cartoon pieces for my simpler suncatchers. I can find cheap pieces of glass at sales and all around, normally it is thin mirror tiles that have aged and the mirroring is going bad, so I get them really cheap.

Then what I do is cut out a paper cartoon of the pieces, transfer that onto the mirror and then cut and grind that mirror down to where it matches the patter perfectly. Once I have all the pieces cut and ground, I then lay them out on a patter to make sure everything lines up right. Once I am happy with that I put felt buttons on the bottom of the glass so that when I place it on the glass I am going to mark and cut, there is no chance it will scratch that glass.

Then I have this perfect, rigid pattern that I can duplicate very easily. Then I store the pieces for that one specific suncatcher in a small plastic storage bag.

I store my originals for my small suncatcher patterns in sleeves that go into a three ring binder. When I am ready to produce some of a pattern I pull out the sheet, place it on my copier and make a copy, then back into the book it goes. Easy peasy!

If I ever break one of those glass pattern pieces, I just make a new one.

Doing it this way, I save myself a LOT of time in production.

Always store your patterns in a dry location. If you are working in a basement, put a dehumidifier down there, not only for your patterns but your tools as well. If you are storing them in containers, make sure your containers are resting above the floor so that they will stay dry in the event your basement floods.

Chapter 3

Efficiency For The Win

Anytime you can work smarter and not harder, you are ahead of the game! Remember, time is money.

Once you have flipped that switch to wanting to start making money with your art and craft you have to start thinking about efficiency in your "workplace".

Many people are limited in the amount of room that they have to work while a few are blessed with an abundance of room. No matter the size of your work area you want to start thinking about the "ergonomics of motion" in relation to your work area.

In other words, is your grinding station near your cutting area and are you able to have a wash area somewhere near there? Where is your work table(s) in relation to where you store your glass, foil, lead, solder and other sundries.

If you are having to do a lot of walking to do all the stages of the production process, is there a way you could modify your work area to streamline it better?

Pattern Pieces or No Pattern Pieces?

Earlier I discussed a technique that I use where I work off of the original pattern and place the glass on top and cut, allowing for the heart of the lead or the appropriate amount for copper foil method.

I am able to do this 95% of the time until I get into glass that is too opalescent and that I can not see through. But I have been doing this off and on since 1988 so I have some practice.

This is not a method I even teach my students, because when they are first learning it would make it too hard in my opinion. Once they have practiced and mastered the basics, then they can start trying to do something like this.

Until you know instinctively how much to remove for lead or foil, it is too easy to cut the pieces wrong. If it is only one or two pieces that is one thing, but if you are dealing with a pattern that has for instance a couple of hundred or more pieces in it, that could make for a very frustrating project if you find that 50% of your glass needs either re-cut or ground down.

Since I am able to do this, it makes the process more efficient for me, thereby making me more money on that project.

I would suggest that you try this method because you will never excel in new areas if you do not try them and practice them.

Size Does Matter

As a general rule of thumb the larger your sheet of glass the more you can control your waste factor.

When you think about it, if you have a 12 inch by 12 inch piece of glass and you have to cut out several odd shapes, it could take up that whole piece of glass and if you were to weigh that glass after it was finished and weigh the scraps that are left over, you could find yourself with a 50% waste factor.

Versus you have a larger piece of glass and you are able to lay it out more efficiently, say for instance along the base of that larger sheet. Now you have maybe a 20% waste factor.

30% may not sound like a lot of savings, and it might only be a savings of 10% which sounds even less, but it all adds up. The less amount of waste you have, the more money you make on that project. And in turn you have more glass available for future projects.

Make Those Scraps Count

I have large and small bins to sort my glass. The large bins are in the neighborhood of 24 inches deep by 48 inches tall, they will vary in their width. Then my smaller bins are 12 inches deep by 12 inches tall and they vary in their width. Perhaps even some smaller bins as well.

This allows me to store large full sheets of art glass as well as "unit" sizes of glass and my cut offs.

Below my cutting table I have multiple boxes for my "other scrap". I generally sort it by size and type. I keep all my iridescent together and then try to sort my other scraps into three other sizes.

Why do I keep my scrap? Well, sometimes I am able to use it in projects. Then other times I can sell the scrap by the pound. If you use a "If it fits it ships" box from the USPS you can readily send out 5 to 20 pounds of scrap at a time to buyers.

Keep the price down, maybe $2 to $5 per pound depending upon what you are selling. Iridized will sell for more and common glass that are very small in size will sell for less.

But there is almost always a market. Another stained glass artist, or someone that does mosaic work, maybe a wood worker that likes to incorporate some glass into their work etc...

Another thing you can do with your scrap is to donate it to a local school's art department. And if you want to, they will give you a tax credit letter. Most schools are 501c3, non-profits. You tell them what it is worth and they will give you that tax credit letter for the amount you want.

There is very little that I throw away.

Now with that said, if you do not have a plan for making money with that scrap don't let it pile up on you. Because then you start affecting your work area and your efficiency because of the clutter.

Don't be a "glass hoarder". Make money off of your scraps!

Chapter 4

Production

Making "stuff" is a lot of fun. Getting paid to make "stuff" is even better!

Now it is time to actually produce your pieces. We have talked about efficiency in your work area and the importance to control your waste factor in glass, but you also have to consider other areas as well.

I try to source my materials as "local" as possible, at the very least I try hard to make sure that the materials I am using are produced in the USA for the most part. Sometimes though I have to used imported glass or other sundries because they are a higher quality than I can get locally. Or the item is just not available locally.

This is important for a few reasons. First and foremost, today's consumer is more savvy in regards to products that are "Made in the USA". And there are a good number of people that care about that aspect.

When I market my products they know immediately that these products were made in my studio. And they also know that I try to source my materials locally. This is good for marketing.

The second reason it is good is because it helps keep our USA supply chain vibrant. Manufacturers stay in business when there is a demand for their product. Wholesalers stay in business when there is a demand. And local studios stay in business when we do business with them.

Personally I have several wholesale accounts with major distributors that saves me on my cost of materials, and every dollar saved is money made. Even if you do not qualify for a wholesale discount you can still shop around and ask for discounts.

There are numerous vendors I buy specific items from that I can buy cheaper but pass on other items that cost me too much.

Another important issue is quality. Sometimes spending a few extra cents or dollars can mean the difference between making a superb product versus a sub par product.

Multiples Versus One at a Time

There are a number of suncatcher patterns I have that I will only produce when I am ready to do several at a time, unless they are being special ordered by a customer. And when they are a special order I normally add a small surcharge for that service, something in the order of $5 extra for most of my suncatchers. Because usually they are wanting a specific color and I may already have 12 of that item and know I do not want to make any more, so will only do that one special order.

I am able to keep my selling price down on simpler suncatchers by "mass producing" them. What is nice is that I can also use up a bunch of my scrap many times when doing these multiples.

Say for instance my small cross suncatcher.

I set up my strip cutter or plug in board system and then pick out about 12 different kinds of glass and cut out strips from them.

Then I set up my plug in board system and cut down those strips to the two different lengths. Normally I have 2 jig setups on the board so I can feed some in for the one length and then for the other length.

By doing it this way, I can quickly knock out enough pieces to assemble 36 crosses.

Since they are straight cuts, and generally I pick glass that does not have a huge amount of texture, I do not have to grind them at all.

Then I pick out 36 random nuggets to place in the center of the cross. Then I foil it all. And then I assemble them all.

Normally I will set up a "jig" which is some cork board with a copy of the pattern on top of it, and use thumb tacks to create the area that I can just slide the pieces into and they are held into place for me to tack solder. Then I tin and finish up the soldering.

Doing multiples at one time is the most efficient way of producing items to keep them at a certain price point. And you get to have a variety for customers to choose from.

When you do them one at a time, you have to charge more, as there is more time invested overall in the production process.

Even on my more complex suncatcher patterns I will wait until I only have 1 or 2 of them left and then make up another 6 to refill my stock.

Custom Orders

I am going to explain to you the way I handle the process of a custom order. And this has worked very well for me in the almost three decades since I first started doing stained glass work.

When a customer contacts me I get a little bit of information up front.

Do they have an idea of design? Perhaps some specific design elements? For instance maybe they know they want some beveled glass, and a couple of roses.

Then I find out the approximate size. Is it going to hang in the window or be trimmed in more permanently? Is it for an operable door? For instance a front door or kitchen cabinet. I always try to find out a budget up front as this affects the design.

From there I let them know I will do up a sketch and price it out for them, I will get into pricing structure in chapter 6. Always sign your sketches.

I then get back a hold of them and show them the sketch and the price for producing that piece along with any other charges there may be. You might have to go yourself and measure, or create a template of an opening (never assume a window is square). Is the customer picking it up or are you going out to install it?

Then I let them know that once they are ready to proceed I require 25% down. This gets me to where I will do a full sized drawing and the glass selection process begins once that drawing is approved.

Have them come to you if you can to pick out glass. And hopefully you have the glass in stock otherwise are you going to take them with you to a studio to pick out glass? That could cause you some problems.

I have worked with clients via email and social media messaging to send them photos of glass, when they were not available to come to me directly. But I always told them that the pictures do only so much to show the true color and characteristics of the glass. Normally I will put the glass in a window sill so that sunlight can come through it and they get a better look at the glass that way.

Then I ask for another 50% down to initiate production. This invests the customer 75% into the project. They are far less likely to get cold feet or just not pick up and pay for the piece when it is finished. And in addition at this stage if you have priced your project properly you are well beyond paying for your materials and time, you are actually making some profit. This reduces your risk of loss on projects immensely.

When I am showing them the sketch and giving them pricing, I make sure to let them know the stages of 25% down, 50% down and balance. Balance due upon pick up or delivery.

Materials

Quality materials really do make the difference in not only the finished product but in your ability to create pieces efficiently.

One prime example is copper foil. Many of the cheaper brands of copper foil are not only thinner copper but the adhesive is not as good as the better quality brands of copper foil. Which means that using the better brand of copper foil gives you greater success at making it stick the first time and if you have to reposition the tape you can do so more than once and it will continue to stick.

If you have ever had issues with "crud" showing up on your soldered areas, either miter joints in lead work or your solder lines in copper foil work, that can many times be attributed to low quality solder and/or flux.

The cheaper brands of solder tend to have impurities in it that end up bubbling to the top once melted, as does the cheaper brands of flux.

Another example of poor quality can be found in glass nuggets. What you will tend to find in cheaper glass nuggets is that some of the colors are actually painted and not solid color that is within the glass itself. The easiest way to test this is to take a razor blade and scratch on the flat side of the nugget. You will usually find the colors that are faked are red, pink and lavender.

You never want to use painted nuggets in a piece because that paint will deteriorate over time. Whomever is purchasing the item you have made expects the colors to stay rich and as true as the day they bought it.

Try to source your materials local. Most of the time when you first start out trying to make money doing stained/art glass work you are still purchasing from retailers since you do not qualify for wholesale accounts. It is very tempting to find the absolute cheapest materials, many times ordering online and having them shipped to you, so that you can obtain the most amount of profit possible. But the issue with that mentality is that the "local" vendors are very important to the overall supply chain, which is something you will realize once you get to the point of having a retail location of your own.

I look at the overall pricing for materials I order and if the pricing is close and within reason I try my best to spend my money with companies that are as local as possible and making sure to buy as much USA made products as possible. Even though I am only one small studio I feel it is important to do my part to keep my local supply chain as viable as possible. So if I come across an item that would cost me $5 and is imported from abroad versus the same item that will cost me $6 but is made in the USA, I purchase the higher priced one. At the end of the day I am still going to make a tidy profit because I am pricing my work appropriately.

I use the USA as my example here because that is where I live, but the same holds true to wherever you live in the world. Attempt to source your materials as local as possible.

In regards to lead came I prefer to work with stick lead versus rolled lead. Normally I will work with three different sizes of lead H came in my pieces; 1/8", 3/16" and 1/4".

A factor in regards to the choice of lead came you work with will be it's antimony. Antimony is a chemical element found in nature as stibnite, a gray metalloid that is lustrous. The higher the percentage of antimony the "stiffer" the lead is to work with.

Lead came that is made today versus the first examples of lead came in stained glass windows has multitudes greater tensile strength. This means that panels made today with lead came, when properly constructed and maintained, have the opportunity to last more than a century without the need for repair or restoration, possibly even onwards of two centuries. Only time will tell in regards to those numbers.

In your marketing you should let people know about how you utilize local materials as many consumers find this information important and can sometimes make the difference between them choosing your studio versus someone else's studio.

I plan on publishing in the future a reference book with information on the major suppliers, wholesalers and manufacturers of products for the stained / art glass industry.

Chapter 5

Safety

When you live and breath safety, your body, mind and appendages will thank you for it!

Safe working practices should be observed at all times, when we let our guard down is when we or others get hurt. Once you have gotten into the habit of working safely it just becomes second nature to you.

Every morning when I go into my studio I vacuum the floor and brush off my work areas. All it takes is one sliver of glass that you do not see to send you to the hospital to get some stitches.

I also make sure to have a smoke detector in my studio area, it is far too easy to leave a soldering iron on and forget all about it. Best case scenario is that you go down the next morning, see what happened and kick yourself in the rear end and have to clean off and re-tin your soldering iron tip. Worst case scenario is the smoke detector goes off.

In addition to the smoke detector I also have a carbon monoxide detector since I do a lot of torch work as well.

I am discussing a few of these safety issues in this chapter as it will especially apply if you end up teaching classes which will be discussed in a future chapter.

Getting The Lead Out

Remember, you are working with materials that contain lead. Solder will have varying amounts of lead and then of course lead came itself has a high amount of lead content.

Never smoke or eat when you might have lead contamination on your fingers. It is easy to forget that you have been handling lead and just reach over and grab a bite of your sandwich.

Think about getting your blood lead levels checked every year if you are active in doing this type of work, or perhaps every other year.

There are various soaps that are designed to more efficiently remove heavy metal dust, lead and contaminants from the skin and hands. Just do an internet search and you will find several good products out there in the market place.

I like to save my scraps of solder and reshape them into solder bars so I get my monies worth out of them. The only sorting I do is to make sure that I do not put lead free solder scraps in the scraps that contain lead.

As for my lead, I save mine until time to take to a local lead reclamation center. Again, you can do an internet search for centers that are close by and if that does not pan out give a local salvage yard a call and tell them what you have and see what they suggest.

I just do not like to put my scraps into the trash where they will wind up in a landfill.

Glass Can Bite!

The vast majority of us that do art glass and stained glass work can swap stories of times we got "bit" by our glass.

It is always a good rule of thumb to wear gloves when handling glass and during all stages of production. I tend to gravitate towards the rubber/plastic coated work gloves.

They are pretty light weight and I can still get the tactile feed back I need when handling, cutting, grinding and assembling the project.

If I am soldering I will usually wear a pair of tight fitting rubber gloves like you would use when cleaning dishes or for other general clean up. I put a little bit of talcum powder in them to help them come off easier and I can re-use them many times this way. These keep the flux and small solder splatters off of my hands.

For assembly if I am working with lead came I have one specific pair I use so that the lead contamination stays on just that one pair.

When you are taking glass in and out of the glass bins you use to store them in, make sure you are wearing gloves. It only takes the blink of an eye to gouge out a nice chunk of flesh from one of your hands.

If you have the glass stacked outside of your storage area, make sure you are aware of where it is. It is very easy to kick that piece or small stack with the end of your foot and nothing good can come of that.

Warnings And Lead Disclosures

You have to keep in mind that you are now making a consumer product. I am not a lawyer, so you may wish to seek the advice of a lawyer versed in these things, but I can tell you that disclosures are important.

I use a sales price tag that I buy in bulk, the tags are 1 3/4 inch long by 1 3/32 inch wide, and they have string loops for attaching to your product.

On those tags I print my information for marketing purposes and warnings. I use a return address label that is 2/3 inch tall by 1 3/4 inch wide. On that label I basically print something on the left side that states who it is made by, which I use my website url for that information. Then add in a couple of bullet points about my services and a contact phone number.

Then on the back is the disclaimer and warning. For me I wanted to make sure that folks understand that the product contains lead and is not meant for children.

When I make an item that is lead free then I can just mark that out on the tag and just keep the "Not meant for children" warning.

On my website where people go to look over my offerings I also have a link to a page that describes my "Terms of Sales and Lead Disclosure". This link appears on every single page of product that I have for sale.

Wear Goggles At All Times

Remember, your eyes are easily damaged from issues such as; glass flicking up from grozing or grinding, glass particles coming up from the use of diamond blade saws, running a score, soldering and so on...

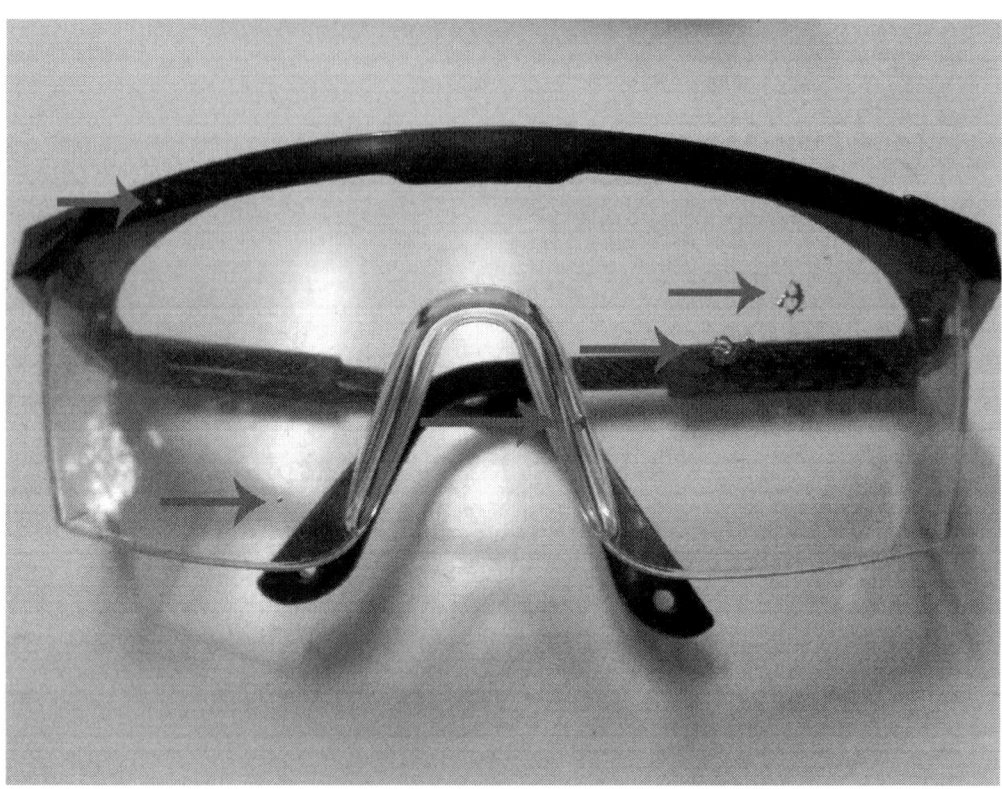

This is a picture I like to show people in regards to the need to use safety glasses, and I actually keep this pair in my studio to show any students I teach.

Those arrows are pointing out were solder splattered up. I have been doing this type of work off and on since 1988 and this was the worst example that I have ever had happen. No matter how "good" you think you are you can not control all the variables.

Had I not been wearing these safety goggles I may very well of had some permanent damage to my left eye.

So what does this have to do with being able to make money doing glass work? Simple. If you injure yourself you are going to have down time and down time makes you lose money. And there is almost always some out of pocket expense involved as well. So think of it as a savings plan for your success!

Chapter 6

Selling Price And Charges

Only YOU can short change yourself. Know your market and set your price accordingly. The right price can be the difference between making money and loosing money.

Price. That is the one common question that most beginners have in regards to their work. There are numerous "formulas" out there which I will share with you one that works well for me. But at the end of the day it will be up to you to take this information and adapt it so that you price your work properly and make the most amount of profit possible.

I will discuss several factors in this chapter in regards to pricing and how to determine the best price possible for your work.

A mindset that many get into initially when they start charging for their work is that if they "break even" on what their cost to produce the items are, then they are happy. You have to move past that line of thinking and look at ways to gain profit and maximize that profit.

Learn Your Market

With the advent of the internet and the way society is so connected now it is pretty easy to go online and find websites for stained glass studios in your area and outside your area as well.

How many other studios are there in your area? If there are few or none at all that is a plus to you as you are now the "local authority". If there are several in the area, you can go and check them out if they have a retail location. This way you can get an idea for what they are selling pieces for and the quality of their work.

Some people will frown at the idea of "pricing the competition", but that is just silly. A strong business understands their competition and that is how they stay competitive. I like to let me clients know that I can guarantee that I am not the cheapest out there but I am also not the most expensive either.

I do not like to put down my competition to a potential client, but I do like to educate them in what they should look for and ask about when considering a studio. When they feel comfortable with me, they spend money with me.

The time that you spend now in learning your market will pay dividends in the long run and you will be a better business person because of that knowledge.

Quality Matters

I can not count the number of times I have seen work being produced that was so far below par it was amazing and on top of that they were charging and receiving premium payment for that level of work. Generally that happens in markets where there are few choices.

You are now stepping into creating consumer products and you should always be mindful of "honing" your skills and making sure you are giving your customer the best quality possible for their money.

When you get known in your area for quality work that in itself will be some of your most effective marketing.

I try to develop and execute pieces that can be handed down from one generation to the next. With that said there is a difference between the life expectancy of a suncatcher versus for instance a full sized panel that has been properly produced and reinforced.

Producing quality products starts with quality materials. That is why I try to use good foil from companies that produce them to have the best adhesion possible and the copper is a bit thicker than the cheap stuff. I also try to utilize good quality glass that is manufactured in the USA and avoid some of the cheap and brittle glass that comes from abroad. Now with that said there is also some imported glass that is top notch and very specialized which you can not find produced in the USA.

I will be endeavoring to put together a resource guide for good quality tools and materials in a future publication. In the interim if you have questions in this area feel free to contact me. You can go to my website for contact information and my contact information is also at the start of this book.

You should always strive to learn proper techniques to be able to produce better and better quality products for your consumers. All of us, myself included, have areas we can get better in and learn something new.

Formula For Success

It will take you time to develop the right formula for pricing out work and even then you need to have some flexibility and consider all the factors in front of you.

Is this a first time and probably only one time customer? Is this a repeat customer or likely to become one?

You also have to have some sort of formula you go by in your pricing, otherwise you wind up with pricing that is confusing to customers. The last thing you want to have happen is to become inconsistent in your pricing and your customer feels like they are getting "ripped off". Trust me when I tell you that they will most likely not tell you that is how they feel, but they will tell everyone they know, and that will hurt you in the long run.

And something to remember is that it is a lot harder to go up in price versus going down. Sure, you do not want to scare people off with absurdly priced items, but if you do your due diligence this should not happen. And it gives you the opportunity to create "specials" for holidays, repeat customers, etc...

Later on in the book I will be discussing how to calculate out your cost to produce in relation to your retail asking price.

For my small suncatchers a good average price of $5 per piece of glass that is in the design is workable. Perhaps your market can only handle $3 per piece, only you will know that once you get going. From there you might add a few dollars if you do some really neat wire work, or the cost of a bevel, jewel or other sundry.

As an example, I have a simple cross suncatcher that has two pieces of glass that overlap each other and a nugget in the center. I wanted something for the religious market and wanted its price point to be low. For craft fairs and such having a few $10 items is good, there have been many times that I made my booth rental fees just on those little $10 items, allowing all of my other sales to provide me the "profit".

I do some smaller panels in copper foil but generally use the leading technique to produce my actual panels.

When creating a larger panel there are generally two main charges you look at and that is a price per piece and a square footage charge. The square footage charge will normally take care of all of your costs to produce the panel and is normally in the $25 to $35 per square foot range. This goes up if you are using exotic or more costly materials, say for instance Dichroic or imported hand blown glass.

Then you will count out the pieces and multiply them by $3 to $5 each, again it really depends on the complexity of the design. If it is a straight forward geometric which you can knock out a lot faster than a piece that has many inside and outside curves, you will want to be in that lower range. Designs that are more complex require a higher charge.

So lets say you have a panel that is 18 inches wide by 24 inches tall, rectangular, and it has 65 pieces of glass in it, mostly geometric, but it also has 4 bevels in it.

Here is how that one would play out in pricing.

18 x 24 divided by 144 = your square feet which is 3 square feet even.

3 square feet x $25 per square foot is $75

65 pieces at $3 per piece is $195

4 bevels. Each cost you $2.50. I like to double my money so that makes them $5 each in what you charge your customer which = $20

Now are you going to do just a regular zinc metal frame? If so you should figure out your cost of the zinc and mark it up by two times like you did the bevels. So lets say that works out to you charging your customer $10 which would be a good minimum charge.

Or do you have the ability to offer custom wood framing? If so, only you know what your cost is per linear foot and how long it takes you to do the framing. Generally speaking $5 per linear foot with a $35 minimum is a good price range to be in for this kind of service.

So lets assume the person is going with a wood frame.

SQ Foot Chg = $75

Piece Chg = $195

Bevels = $20

Frame = $35

Total Due = $325 which makes your average per square foot charge $108 per square foot.

Many beginners would look at this pricing and say "No way, I can't get that for this piece". In fact, you can and that is a fair price range for an art/stained glass artisan, providing the quality of your work is there.

I use formulas like the one above because it really helps when a design is more complicated than others and in turn it helps me adjust accordingly.

If you were to look at the range of prices that studios end up charging per square foot, they really do have a large range. Anywhere from $75 a square foot to several hundred dollars a square foot. Many are in the $175 a square foot range for a decently complex design.

With time and first hand experience you will gain the knowledge of what designs will take longer than others and will be able to adapt on the fly.

Normally when I quote a price to a client I let them know it is based on the sketch I have done for them and the complexity of the design and then ask them if the pricing is good.

Do not start the conversation out immediately with the option of reducing complexity to lower the cost of the piece, otherwise you will lose money in the long run because it is human nature to want to save money and if presented with that option from the get go your client is more likely to say "OK, lets simplify it a bit so I can save money.".

You are going to run into those clients that are adamant that they can get the same work performed for much, much less somewhere else. Many times that is part of their negotiating process, just remember this is why you are asking a fair amount so that you might have a little wiggle room if you so choose.

Installation And Service Calls

Installation of panels can be tricky at the best sometimes, you will learn to expect the unexpected. When you start doing installations you are going to want to check into an insurance policy called "General Liability". Basically this insurance covers any damage you do to a home or property during your installation or resulting from your installation. These policies can vary in cost so it is best to get several quotes.

Generally speaking a one million dollar policy is sufficient. It really depends on your average clientele. Also you can get special one time policies written for specific jobs. If you end up doing some high end or commercial installations the client may require you have specific coverage's.

When I do custom work I offer the ability, for a charge, to have me come out and do the measurements, take some photos and create a template if need be for the window that the piece is going to be put into.

I will explain to the customer that I will be more than happy to work off of their measurements, their templates etc... but that if there are any unforeseen variations that cause the piece not to fit properly and I have made it exactly to their specifications, their will be a charge to fix the issue. Normally this will prompt them to put the monkey on my back.

An average service call charge within a nominal distance from your studio might be $35 to $50. This way it is not outrageous but it takes care of your gas and a little bit of your time.

You should always have paper with you, rolled butcher type paper is good as is a rolled craft type paper, so that you can create a template if need be. In addition, I like to keep a large piece of cardboard with me as well for the same reason.

Take a camera with you or use your phones camera if it takes good enough photos so that you can take photos of the interior and exterior of the installation area.

Measure the opening width and height. Make sure to check in three places for each. On a side that would mean a measurement at the top, middle and bottom. On a top or bottom side that would mean a measurement at the left, middle and right.

Next you are going to want to have a carpenters square with you so that you can check the installation area for being in square or not.

If the measurements are true and the opening is square, all you really need to do is write down the measurements.

If they are not, that is when you will write down all the measurements and then make a template of the opening. Where this is really important is when you are making the panel to be a snug fit into the installation area and it is going to be trimmed in to hold it into place. By that, I mean using wood trim board and placing on the front facing surface of the edges of the panel after it has been put into place. This basically sandwiches the panel against the existing glass and holds it into place and offers an area for your rebar to be notched into, I will get more into reinforcement later on in the book.

When you have made a template because the opening is out of square you also should notate the measurements of how "off square" the area is, just for future reference. Too much information is better than not enough, you will also want to notate top and bottom.

And if there are mullions in the window, those bars that go up and down and across the inside of the window, you will want to measure their placement. This is important for the design stage as you may be able to incorporate some solder/lead lines that correspond with some if not all of those mullions, making them less apparent.

Chapter 7

Where And How To Sell

Three most important things about where to sell are; Location, Location, Location.

There are numerous avenues for finding places to sell your works and I am going to discuss the pros and cons of several types that I have utilized myself in the past as well as issues to look out for and questions to ask.

You will find the need to invest a few dollars in some equipment for setup as well as marketing. I will be discussing marketing ideas and practices further in to the book.

I started out small, normally looking for events that would accommodate a 10 foot by 10 foot area. This allowed me to set up a couple of folding tables and my canopy with "walls" to display my panels and suncatchers. Then I moved up to utilizing spots that were 10 foot by 20 foot as my stock of available items increased and dictated the need for more room.

There will be some discussion about selling online and through social media as well.

Must Haves

In regards to doing craft fairs, farmers markets and the like, there are some items you will have to get for setting up that will just make your life a lot easier and help you create a good looking set up.

Initially I would suggest you use the following shopping list;

Folding Tables. QTY 2 - 5 foot tables, QTY 1 - 4 foot table

Canopy. QTY 1 - 10 foot by 10 foot canopy. Get a good quality one, you will probably spend around $100 for this. Save your receipt because depending on where you buy it from you may be able to return and exchange it up to 90 days after purchase if something goes wrong with it, say for instance a rip in the fabric.

Weights. QTY 4 for each leg of the canopy. You can make your own with a 5 gallon bucket and half a bag of quick set cement. Sinking a 2 x 4 with an eyelet screw in one end.

Power. Qty 1 grounded 100 foot extension cord. Qty 1 power strip. You might also invest in a portable power supply. I have one for when I am somewhere and there is no power available. Mine is a battery power supply. You could use a generator, but be aware that some places will not let you set up a generator due to fire codes or they are just too noisy and the exhaust is not wanted. With my battery powered portable power supply I am able to run my cash register and keep my tablets and phone charged and can even plug in one of my LED light strips.

Lights. Qty 2 LED light strips, I use 4 foot ones. There may be times you are setup outside and the show runs into the dark hours of the evening, you do not want to be the one setup that has no light, people will just walk by you.

Money Security. You should get either a cash box that is lockable or a cash register. My cash register cost me $99 and I got it from one of the big retailers. You can also get a lockable cash bag from your bank for a fee.

A Second Canopy. Most setups give you a 10 foot by 10 foot space, so getting 1 canopy that is a 10 by 10 should be sufficient. One thing that I realized after a month or so of doing these kinds of shows is that I would need to start getting a double sized space when setting up. Which meant that I also bought a second canopy. Sometimes it is used, sometimes I leave that extra area open, it just depends on how I need to set up. When you are setting up in an inside venue you may find you still want to use a canopy but just put up the framework and leave off the covering. This allows you to attach display panels and hang items.

Display Panels. These are the panels you use to attach to your canopy and attach suncatchers and other hanging items on. What I have found works best are "cattle panels". You buy these at most any farm and ranch supply store. They measure 4 foot by 16 foot. When I go to buy one I take a pair of bolt cutters with me and cut them in half, in relation to the length. So I wind up with a 4 foot by 8 foot panel. These are the perfect size to stand on end and attach to some of the perimeter of my canopy frame work. They can also be attached to each other to form stand alone columns to hang items off of. They are very versatile in how they can be used. And being galvanized they last a long time with no rusting. Below you will see two pictures of ways that I have used them myself.

Chairs. A couple of metal folding chairs will last you a long time and don't take up much area when packed away.

Cooler. Get a decent enough sized cooler to take with so that you have cold water and snacks or sandwiches. I like to patronize local food vendors when they are at the show, but at the end of the day it is about me making money. And I can save money by packing a few sandwiches and have lots of good cold water to keep hydrated.

Bungee Cords. The little ones work great on putting together your cattle panels and attaching them to your canopy frame as well as tarps.

Cleaning Supplies. Keep a new roll of paper towels and ammonia free window cleaner with you. During the slow time when there is no one in your area you can get up and clean items. Clean pieces market better than dirty ones.

Tarp. Get one or two tarps that will be large enough to cover your canopy and form "walls". You will keep these with just in case it starts raining. Also, if you are doing a show that requires more than one day set up and you are going to leave your items there you really want to secure them as much as possible.

Other Helpful Items To Get

Fan. When I am doing an outside show where I know it may be getting hot and that I will have electric available I will normally take two decent sized fans with me. One is to help keep me cool all day long and the other is to help keep my patrons cool when they come into my area to browse and buy. They really do appreciate that little touch.

Jumper Cables. Have a set with you just in case you leave a door open too long and drain your battery, or to help someone else out. I am a big believer in karma.

Table Cloth. A table cloth on your display tables makes things look nice. But try to keep it neutral and avoid white. White ones get ruined so fast from stains. And if it is too "bright" or "busy" that can actually detract from your merchandise.

Insurance

I am not an insurance sales person or professional, so please take this information as suggestions only and do your due diligence and talk to a professional about your particular needs.

Some events and venues will require you to carry insurance. Generally speaking they will have this requirement in the application that you fill out, but you should always ask them about it as well when making your initial inquiries.

Some of those events and venues will have sources that you can go to for those coverage's, others figure you will either already have it or know where to go to get it.

You can go online a do a search query with the keywords "special events insurance" and find lots of resources and contact information. Call around and get quotes.

You may find that you want to have what is called a General Liability insurance. This will help cover you if you if for example you are teaching classes and someone gets hurt, or someone comes to pick out glass for a project and gets hurt. Just keep in mind though that if you are doing this out of your home that could be a reason for them not to pay, so you have to make sure they understand this is an in-home business. And vice versa, a home owners policy may not pay since you are operating a "business" in your home.

Farmers Markets

Farmers markets are a great way for you to get out and meet customers that you would not normally have had the opportunity to get in front of before.

Many of them will have what are called "daily vendor" spots that you can set up on with short notice and do not have to commit to several weeks by paying ahead for all of them, it is literally set to where you pay for that day and sell that day. This may be a way for you to find out if a particular farmers market has good enough foot traffic.

Then they will have their seasonal vendors that pay for several weeks in advance and normally this allows them to reserve a specific spot. This is how I have set up in the past at these kinds of events as it gave my customers a feeling of reliability that I would always be in that one spot on a particular day.

Generally there is a flat fee that is paid for the spot and then some farmers markets will take a percentage of the days sales, normally in the range of 5%. When you think about it, that is fair, especially when the market manager is doing a good job in marketing and advertising the market which in turn generates a decent amount of foot traffic for you and the other vendors. In smaller towns and cities the market may not even charge for you to come out and sell.

Just keep in mind that in outdoor events such as these you need to keep an eye on the weather. If there is a significant chance for rain during the time I was going to do one, I would not go because it just was not worth the risk of damaging product.

If you do get caught in bad weather you need to have those tarps with you so that you can close up your canopy area quickly to reduce that risk of damage to your items.

Craft Fairs And Selling Events

When I am researching a craft fair or selling event I like to ask several questions of the person putting on the event to determine if it is worth my time and money.

I will ask them; How many years has this event been going on? What was the approximate foot traffic for last year? How and when are you advertising this event? If this is an overnight/multi-day event is the area secured and is there security patrolling the area? Is electric available and if so does it cost extra? Is Wi-Fi available and if so is there a charge to access it? Do you provide tables and chairs? How early can I come in and set up and can I set up the day before?

If they are unable or unwilling to answer those simple questions then I usually will not do the event. In addition, if it is a first year event I normally will not do those unless they are close by and relatively cheap to do, as they normally have very low foot traffic since they are not established yet.

What I have found is that for an established event it normally will run in the $50 to $75 range per day. If someone is asking $100 or more per day for an event they had better be able to convince me that they have heavy foot traffic.

Events that charge for admission I tend to also avoid since they have much lower foot traffic. By the same token, those people going to an event where they have to pay to get in are generally going to spend money there. But is it the right type of event where they will be interested in your product? I have had mixed results with those events.

Also I tend to avoid carnivals. "Family" friendly events like that generally mean that there are families going there for them and their kids to go on rides and eat food, so that is where the bulk of their money goes. I have very rarely made any profits on those types of events.

Flea Markets

Flea markets can be risky to put your items into for a variety of reasons so make sure to ask lots of questions. My suggestion would also be to ask them what their busiest day is for sales and then make sure to go by there on that day and "mill around" for awhile to see for yourself what kind of foot traffic they have.

Most flea markets will not take responsibility for broken or stolen merchandise so make sure to clarify that with them prior to signing an agreement.

Make sure to have an inventory sheet with you when you set up or drop off items and have them sign off on what as being dropped off. When I have gone this route I made sure to unpack the items I took that day and then I took a photo of them to show they were there and their condition. Go in once a month, normally if they close off their "books" on the last day of the month I would go in that next morning and check my inventory. This will keep you on top of any discrepancies between what they say they sold and what they pay you for that month.

Depending on how you are set up there may be a charge for a booth fee plus a percentage of sales or if they are scattering your items out and about there is normally a percentage of sales fee. Those percentages will normally go anywhere from 25% to 35% on average.

Remember, the higher their percentage, the less you are making. Unless you end up marking up the items that go into their store. Here is the issue with that. If you have a customer buy from the flea market at one price and then find that you are selling to the public directly for a different and lower price they may very well come to you wanting a refund of the difference. To them they don't understand why you should be marking up your items that way. All that can lead to is bad PR for you. These are things you need to consider because you are no longer just trying to make a few dollars here and there, you are trying to make a living doing this, that means your sales efforts are going to be a lot more noticeable than ever before.

For me, when I did flea markets I put in select items that I knew I was making more money on because I could knock them out quicker and had less hard costs in, so my profit margin was bigger to start with and I could take the hit of the commission from the flea market when it sold. I would not mark them up beyond their normal price.

Also, you will want to create your own labels that has your name and contact information on them. This helps you generate custom order sales or sales of other merchandise you don't have on display at that location, and then you have no commission to pay on those items being sold.

Never let a location tell you what you are going to put in and what you are not going to put in. You know your market and what sells better than they do. Never let them talk you into producing special merchandise just for them, that merchandise will end up being so niche that those pieces will most likely not sell as quickly and then you are out the time and materials for them and the flea market has no risk involved at all. That is a win win for them and a lose lose for you.

If they want you to produce specific items for them, figure out a wholesale price and tell them you will sell it to them for that amount so they can mark it up and make money and handle it like you would with any other custom order. Get a percentage down and balance on delivery.

Also ask them about what kind of security they have. Do they have cameras on the premises and signage that states such? If they do, their theft rate will most likely be much smaller.

Only commit to a month by month agreement with them. This way if sales do not perform as expected you can pull your product at the end of the month and move it somewhere else.

Some flea markets allow one day set-ups in their parking lot, so that might be an avenue for you as well. Then you just pay them a flat rate for the day and no commission.

Galleries And Commission Sales

Art galleries can be wonderful opportunities to present your work to the public and more importantly to those in the market for art.

But you have to make sure your bases are covered and that you are making money. As with anywhere you are putting your work into that isn't your own location you need to ask them how they handle damage or theft. Do they have insurance that covers those instances?

Also make sure your commission rate is reasonable. Gallery commissions will generally be between 25% to 50%. So you have to ask yourself if the exposure is worth the cost of placing one or more of your items in the gallery.

Some galleries will let you have the provision that you can still sell your pieces directly and that if you do you can remove them from the gallery with no penalty, just make sure to talk to them about this. When you have an item for sale in a gallery and you still market to the general public, if you have someone that wants to buy from you directly let them know you have to first verify if the piece is still available and never commit to pulling the piece from the gallery until you have payment, as that could ruin your relationship with the gallery if you pull an item more than once only to have the deal fall through and you take it back to them over and over.

Payments

You should always have sufficient change on hand for selling events. Normally I like to have $50 in one's, $50 in five's and $100 in ten's. If you are charging tax you will need to make sure to have a roll of quarters, dimes, nickels and pennies. Otherwise keep your pricing to even numbers and you will not need any coin change.

I do not take personal checks at selling events and the reason why is that if the check bounces it is a headache to get the money back from them. The only time I take checks is when someone is paying down on custom work or if they are sending me a check for giftware and then they know that the item will not be shipped out for 5 business days after it is deposited. This gives my bank plenty of time to notify my if the check bounces.

In regards to credit cards, you need to take them. If you are not taking credit cards you are loosing money, plain and simple. The folks that say otherwise have no clue.

It is so easy nowadays to accept credit cards, there are numerous services out there, including being able to get set up with a merchant account through your bank, but that is expensive.

I personally use one of the online services and if you would like more information about who I use just contact me. But basically there is no contract and the magnetic strip reader is free and works with my smart phone. The software is free. A chip reader does cost, but it is a worthwhile investment, normally they will run $50 to $100 from the service you are using.

And then it is just a flat percentage and sometimes a low transaction fee. So for instance it costs you 3% and .10 cents per transaction. That is well worth it and far cheaper than traditional merchant accounts through your bank.

For me I get my money deposited into my account generally the next business day.

And again, I can guarantee you that you are loosing business if you don't accept them. I am even able to email invoices that my clients who then click a link and pay online, then I ship out product when I get the confirmation it is paid. I have sold internationally this way.

Social Media Sales

I am going to get a little bit more in depth about this later on in my chapter on marketing but I wanted to touch base real quick about this subject.

In today's connected society you can reach a much more vast market than you ever have been able to in the past.

My market is global, my work is as far away as Sweden and The Netherlands. And that is due in part to my utilization of social media to market my work. There is no reason what so ever you can not do the same.

In Summary

It is all about getting your name and knowledge of your products and services out there in front of as many people as possible.

But you have to make sure to do so in a smart way that gives you as much return on investment as possible.

For example, if an event costs you $200 in fees to do that doesn't mean you are making profit once you sell $200 worth of product.

You have to figure in your gas cost, lodging, food etc.. So lets say after all that is said and done you are $350 into the event. You still have to sell more than $350 to start making profit because of the cost to produce the product. So in fact you need to probably sell more like $500 before you are into the profit. These are the kinds of things you need to keep in mind in determining if an event is successful or not.

Another thing to keep in mind is to not get discouraged and pack up early. First off, event coordinators do not like that and will probably not let you attend again if you do that to them. Secondly, you never know who is going to walk up to you and buy from you at the last minute.

I have literally had someone come up to me while I was packing and buy several hundred dollars worth of items from me and had I given up and left early I would not of gotten that money and had the potential to have them as a repeat customer.

Sometimes it is about making contacts, especially once you get into taking custom orders. Many times I have given someone a flier or business card to have them contact me months down the road and order something from me.

So the biggest bit of advice I have for you is to not get discouraged. Keep your passion!

Chapter 8

Make It To Last

"When I make something that I know will be around for numerous generations and possibly even hundreds of years, that excites me!"
~ *Frank Elder II*

We have become a society of "expendable wares". In our efforts to make and provide items to our consumers that are cheaper and cheaper, we have lost sight of quality and longevity of product.

Examples of this can be found everywhere in our daily lives. From electronics to furniture, appliances, doodads and doomawitchies. It is called planned obsolescence and we have allowed ourselves to be conditioned to the inevitable mindset that one day soon, that item will no longer function properly and need to be replaced.

When you are creating these wonderful little works of art for your clients and customers you have to step outside of that mindset and put quality and longevity to the forefront of your production process.

If you do this, you will have repeat customers. You will have customers that sing the praises of your craftsmanship and quality.

When I create an item, even a simple suncatcher I always try to figure out ways that I can make them last as long as possible. And if you get yourself into that kind of mindset where you are always analyzing and looking for new ways to create even better products, it will show in your creations.

Proper Construction Method

It is up to you to determine the proper construction method for the piece you are creating. Will it last longer if it is made with lead came or copper foil? Those are only two examples of various construction techniques available.

This book is not designed to teach you technique, I assume you already have knowledge of various techniques and are just looking for that additional knowledge and insight on how to flip the switch and start making money doing what you love.

But there are limitations to every fabrication technique available, and it is up to you as the artisan to figure out which one is better suited for the application at hand. It is up to you to further your learning and knowledge base, to step outside of your comfort zone and to learn new techniques.

There are those that will argue copper foil will last as long as leaded panels, personally I am not one of those in that camp. I have made and will continue to make many items in copper foil, sometimes that is the only way you can. Take for instance lampshades. It would be pure folly to try and construct a Tiffany style lampshade, for instance a Wisteria replica, in lead. It just is not feasible and will not stand the test of time. You have to construct that piece in copper foil.

But the same can be said for full sized panels. It would be folly to create a large panel, say for instance something that measure 24 inches wide by 48 inches tall in copper foil. It just will not have the strength required to last multiple generations, let alone a century or longer.

I have even heard some folks say things like; "What do I care if it lasts longer than I will live?" or "If it lasts at least 10 years they are getting their monies worth, anything longer is a bonus.".

And that is the wrong mindset to have. When you charge for a product you should do your best to assure that product is going to last as long as possible. Will a suncatcher last 100 years or more? Most likely not without the need for repair or restoration. But, that doesn't mean you should be ok with it only lasting a few years.

Reinforcement

Proper reinforcement is a must for the longevity of any piece and most particularly the larger panels that hang within or are directly installed into windows, entry doors, sidelights, transoms, cabinet doors and such.

There will be times that you may have a customer ask you to put no reinforcement on a piece because they are afraid that it will interfere with the aesthetics of the piece. At the end of the day it is your choice if you do so or not, but it has been my experience that once I properly explained the benefits to adding reinforcement to a piece the client then agrees.

In all the years that I have been doing this kind of work I think there has been perhaps two times that I ended up refusing to do a job because the customer insisted on not having any reinforcement to the piece. One of those was going to be a skylight insert.

The reason I bring up the issue of reinforcement of pieces is because of my mindset of creating pieces that will stand the test of time and give the customer their monies worth.

Even small suncatchers can have their hanging loops attached in such a way that they are less likely to "pull away" from the piece. You just have to take time to analyze the situation, the pattern, and make adjustments accordingly. Have an open mind to doing so.

Chapter 9

Marketing

Artists and businesses that successfully market themselves are the ones that stick around. Word of mouth is very effective but only takes you so far.

Marketing is very different today than it was say 50 years ago. We are a digitally connected society now where the proliferation of information happens in a matter of moments, not a matter of days, months or years.

I am going to discuss some "old school" forms of marketing as well as the modern approaches to marketing using social media.

The one thing you have to keep in mind is that there is no one out there more invested in your success than you! Marketing firms, radio stations and television stations will all talk about the importance of being your "partner" for success, but at the end of the day it is about filling ad spots and taking care of their bottom line.

I have utilized those afore mentioned forms of advertising through out my years as a business owner and while in management of companies I worked for, and the one common denominator that I can tell you held true is that unless you had deep pockets and could commit to a constant and frequent schedule of ads, those ad spots just did not pay off.

There is no reason you can not effectively market your product and services with very little overhead and I am going to explain how you can do that.

Cards And Fliers

The majority of most households today have a computer and printer in them and if you don't personally own those items you will inevitably know a friend or family member that does and can help you out.

Business cards are important, there is no where I go without several in my wallet or automobile. I hand them out every chance I get. And I print my own.

In addition to business cards I also print out my own tri-fold fliers that highlight my custom and repair services as well as my background in this trade.

On those business cards and fliers I make sure people know my website url, my email address and my cell phone number.

If you plan on doing custom work you will want to get out and do some meet and greets with business owners, church staff and such. You never want to leave with just a handshake, those are forgotten within minutes or days. Leaving a business card and a flier helps assure those contacts will remember you when the need arises for your services.

When I am set up at selling events I will have fliers and cards scattered along the numerous tables I have set up and people will pick them up when they are interested and take them with.

I will take a day and drive around with a list of churches, cabinet makers, door manufacturers, interior designers and architects. Then stop in and shake some hands and leave some business cards and fliers.

If you don't feel comfortable printing out your own business cards and fliers there are plenty of services online that can do it for you. Just make sure to shop around. I would also suggest that you have someone you trust to proof read all your copy before actually mass printing them. Many times another persons eyes will see mistakes yours doesn't.

Banners

If you are planning on doing craft fairs, selling events, farmers markets and such, you are going to want to invest in a couple of banners.

There are a lot of online services that offer cost effective options and quick turn around for the creation of those banners. But I would suggest looking local also and here is why.

Many times you can find a local sign maker that will be comparable in price to those online options, sometimes if they are more then it is only by a small amount.

I like to support other local business owners and I always let them know that I am doing so in our conversation when I am getting price quotes from them. I like to let them know that I am actively seeking out local vendors for what I need versus sending my hard earned dollars somewhere else.

This makes a difference most of the time, in fact I find that I normally get some discounts from those small business owners when they know that I am trying to help them pay their bills. It makes them feel important and obliged.

Let me focus on that one word, obliged. This is important because now you also have another "in" for your marketing efforts. When you spend your dollars local and create a relationship with those you are spending your dollars with, they are very apt to retain your information and then either use it themselves or pass it on to others they know that might be able to utilize your product or services.

The majority of the time I find that when I develop that kind of relationship with someone it pays dividends in the long run. There have been times I have left a card and flier with them to end up having someone they referred me to contact me and purchase a substantial amount from me.

I purchased 4 banners from a local vendor, they are about 6 feet wide by 18 inches tall. They have the business name of "Creations By Elder" with a small ".com" just behind it so people know I have a website also. Then there are several bullet points for product and services and my phone number.

When I am set up at a selling event there is a minimum of 1 banner placed on the outside of my canopy, up high on the cattle panels. Normally I have 2 or 3 of them up like this on the sides that can be seen most prevalently. When people are 30 feet away they can see my banners easily and it draws them into my area.

Then I put one banner up on the inside of my main canopy, just behind my small 4 foot table that I have set up to take payments and wrap purchases.

It is all about making sure your "brand" is seen and remembered.

Farmers Markets

These are great events to do and get decent sales as well as sales leads, providing the market has good foot traffic. You should always have a clipboard available to write down someone's information that shows interest in a product or service that you offer when they are not buying right then. This allows you to follow up on that lead later on.

Also, if you are doing custom work you should always have another clip board with your work orders on them. There is no reason you can not take an order while you are there and even get a down payment. At the very least you can get detailed information about their project and follow up with sketches and quotes later.

I am fortunate to have one of my children learning this trade and he normally goes with me on the weekends when I do a show and helps me man the booth, answer questions and sell product.

If you are able to have someone with you to help you man your booth you should take the opportunity once in awhile to walk around and talk to other vendors. Introduce yourself and hand them a card and/or flier. This is called networking and it will pay dividends in the future, trust me.

Other times it also allows me to go around and hand out coupons, which I will address here in a little bit.

Farmers markets have a customer base you are looking for and that is individuals that put importance on locally sourced and handmade products. These are the people that have some money in their pocket and are willing to spend it with you that day if you have something that appeals to them. Which is why you want to make sure to have a broad range of offerings.

It takes me, with my sons help, about 2 1/2 hours to set up and the same amount of time for tear down. So if it starts at 7am we are there at 4:30am to start our setup.

I have literally hundreds of products to put out. Tons of suncatchers, desk art, full sized panels etc... And our set up is a 10 foot by 20 foot booth area. You should plan on about 1 to 1 1/2 hours for a 10 foot by 10 foot area.

Coupons

There are times when I am set up at a selling event that I like to create coupons to hand out that day that helps generate sales.

Most of the time I will create a coupon around a holiday. So for instance if it is getting close to mothers day I will create a "Mother's Day" coupon for something like 15% any purchase for "your mom".

You have to make sure that these coupons are a "call to action". In other words, it prompts the recipient to act upon that offer immediately and not hold onto the coupon to only throw it away later on down the road or get washed when it is forgotten in their laundry.

Let's use that Mothers Day Coupon as an example. Here is a sample of a coupon I would use at a farmers market.

```
┌─────────────────────────────────────────────────┐
│           Creations By Elder                    │
│  ─────────────────────────────────────────      │
│            MOTHER'S DAY SPECIAL                 │
│                                                 │
│         15% OFF any purchase of                 │
│           giftware for your mom!                │
│                                                 │
│       Valid today only, must use before 1pm     │
│  ─────────────────────────────────────────      │
│         XXXXX Farmers Market Coupon             │
└─────────────────────────────────────────────────┘
```
(www.CreationsByElder.com / support@creationsbyelder.com / 479-595-6110)

There are a few important things to note about this coupon.

First, it is branded with the name of my studio and also the name of the event. In case they do not use this coupon that day but still retain it this will remind them where they saw my booth set up at and perhaps the following weekend they will look for me again.

Second, it reminds them about Mother's Day. Who wants to be known as the child that forgot to get something for their mother?

Third, it gives them a significant savings which is more likely to make them use it. But it is not so large that it is eating away at my profit.

Fourth, it is branded with my web url and contact information. Again, they may not use this coupon but might retain it and then when they get time they may very well go check out my website or call/email me to inquire about what other items I may have.

Fifth and most important, it is a call to action. You will see where it says that it is valid only that day and must be used before a certain time. That creates a sense of urgency and is more likely to make them act upon the coupon versus putting it off until next time.

Also when you create a coupon and it does not have a call to action for that day but instead is designed to help generate business down the road, you want to be able to track the metrics of that effort.

I do multiple shows and events. If I have branded my coupon with the event name then I know which events work better for me than others, in follow up coupon marketing.

For me a coupon though is designed to create a call for action on that day, so I generally only make coupons good for that event only.

My business cards and fliers are my marketing material used to hand off to people to use at a later time.

Contact Logs

No matter the source of contact, when I have someone inquire about purchasing a product, having custom work performed or repair and restoration services, I keep a log of who it was, what it was about and their contact information and the date of initial contact.

Then I follow up on that log. I normally write the date I followed up on and a short note. Even if I only left a voicemail I will put (VM) next to that date. Or more specific information.

Some people feel they are being "intrusive" and "bugging" people by doing this, and that is the farthest from the truth and you have to get past that line of thinking. You have to treat each contact as a "gold nugget", because they are worth a lot and that information represents a lot of time and effort on your part to obtain. If you ignore that contact you are shooting yourself in the foot, plain and simple.

There is an old sales analogy that goes something like this. You have to talk to xxx amount of people to get xxx amount of no's before you can get to that one yes. And that is true. It is a percentages game. If you don't make 100 contacts you will never get to those 10 maybes that lead you to those 1 or 2 yes answers.

A contact log is an effective way to make sure you are following up on those hard earned leads. There are many people that will appreciate your follow up.

How often should you follow up? Well that depends on what the conversation was. Did you tell them you would follow up in a specific time frame? If so, you better do so or you lose your credibility.

If there was nothing said about follow up, you need to do so within a few days initially. The longer you wait the greater the chance that they will no longer feel your product or service is something they require.

Vehicle Signage

Vehicle signage is a great way to get the information out about your studio, but you have to keep it simple. The average person viewing vehicle signage will only view it for a few seconds, long enough to get the information if it is concise and to the point, but if it is cluttered and too much to read, they will ignore it.

Vehicle wraps and signage are one of the most cost effective ways to get your information out there, your ROI (return on investment) is much better than say for instance billboards, radio, tv, newspaper etc...

It is estimated that the average American travels about 36 miles per day in their vehicle. This can lead to hundreds or thousands of possible impressions of your information, it really depends upon how densely populated the area is that you are traveling.

I personally have found that the rear of my vehicle is one of the best places for this kind of advertising, as people sitting behind you have more time to read than those driving by.

As a side note though, you will want to make sure that by having such signage on your vehicle you are not giving your auto insurance company an "out" on paying any claims. They may very well have a clause that if your vehicle is being used for business that your personal type coverage will not be valid and that you instead need a rider of some sort or even a commercial policy versus a personal policy.

Signing Your Work

I don't sign all of my work, more specifically my smaller pieces such as sun catchers. Unless I am asked to by my customer, which has happened numerous times.

But I make it a habit to sign my larger work and date them. This does a few things.

First, it adds a perceived additional "value" to the piece. You are after all the artist that created the work and your client may actually insist on this, I have had that happen many times.

Second, it is another form of advertising. When that piece is being displayed somewhere the person viewing it may very well want to order something just like it and if your name is on there they are more likely to look for you specifically.

It should not be an obtrusive signature as that may very well detract from the aesthetics of the piece.

I normally use a diamond engraver to "etch" my name and date on the piece along with sometimes the name of the piece if it is a specifically named piece or in a series. Other times I may paint and fire that same information within the piece. Usually in the bottom right area for consistency.

I have been known to introduce my signature and date to an area within a piece when I am already doing painting and firing in it. For instance in a leaf, trunk of a tree, slope of a hill etc...

Social Media

This is such an underutilized and sometimes misunderstood form of marketing. And trust me there are numerous businesses out there that will try to convince you that for a fee they can make you an overnight success on social media. I tend to avoid those and do all of my own marketing.

Basically what you have to do is get into a mindset that this is another "tool" for you to use, to help you make money.

So many times people are used to going onto their social media platforms to play games and interact with others, day in and day out. So once they start thinking about using those same social media platforms as a form of marketing it is hard for them to get into the proper mindset.

I usually spend a 1/2 an hour to 1 hour every morning using two or three of my social media platforms to announce specials, specific products, services, new client work, classes etc..

I have disciplined myself to this so that I don't waste hours upon hours on social media when instead I could be making product to sell. I figure that optimally when I am creating product to sell I am generating $100 per hour in product. If I am not producing at least $250 worth of product every day when I am not working on client projects, there is something wrong. I can not do that if I am spending my whole day on social media.

There are many "sales groups" in your area you can join and utilize them to post up information daily about your offerings. The key is to join enough of them that you are not just posting in one or two all the time. If you do that you could very well find yourself removed from the groups for "spam". I like to rotate between a lot of groups.

Since I ship all over the country and even internationally, I am part of hundreds if not a couple of thousand selling groups. If you want to keep your business local you should be able to become part of a dozen or more sales groups in your area.

I find that weekends, early morning and evenings are my best times to use my social media. When people are at home or have time to browse.

Also, when you start out using social media to market, don't get discouraged if you don't see interactions immediately. In fact I can guarantee you that it will look like all there are is crickets chirping in the background to start with.

But that doesn't mean that your efforts are not effective. There are many times you will never know who is telling whom about your information. So don't think that your efforts are for naught when you do not see people that "liked/favorited/shared" your posts etc...

Track Your Efforts

The key to any good marketing campaign is to track your efforts. How can you adapt and change your efforts if you don't know what works and what doesn't?

When I get a phone call or email, I always ask people how they found out about me. If I get messaged through social media I also ask that question, you can't assume it is just a post that prompted them to contact you.

I make sure any coupons I create are traceable so I know what events and offers were the most successful.

One of the biggest mistakes that small business owners make in regards to their marketing efforts is to not ask for that information. Again, it just really comes down to "flipping" that switch in your head and creating different and better habits.

Chapter 10

Donations And Family

Helping the community around you as well as friends and family is a wonderful thing but it is easy to start loosing money by doing it the wrong way.

Community involvement is hugely important and I am a firm believer in giving back to the community around you when you can. I love to give pieces to friends and family during the holidays, there is nothing more special than giving someone a gift that you have actually made yourself for them.

Now with all that said, there is a right way and a wrong way to go about it and you can really end up on the wrong side of your balance sheet if you let your heart fully dictate your actions.

Some may find that to be a bit cold hearted but you have to remember, this is now your business. This is how you provide for yourself, your loved ones and family.

I am a firm believer in karma and if you strive to do good in your life it will come back to you ten fold. But that doesn't mean you can't do good and be smart about it and help assure that you continue to stay financially viable and strong.

Donations

I have been doing this type of work for a long time and know many other artists and business owners. And inevitably you will be approached about donations for various causes, local and otherwise.

I will explain to you the method I have developed in handling those inquires. This is a method I have developed over the decades of doing this type of work and have found it to be a fair way to help out various causes and organizations while assuring that I am not going in the hole with my efforts.

Event coordinators have all of the best intentions in the world when they are soliciting donations for their event, but at the end of the day it is about doing what is best for their organization and to help assure they get the most amount of donations possible, and that is understandable.

But you have to remember, and especially when you first start out and are struggling to make ends meet, you are the only one really looking out after yourself.

I have a more in-depth description of how I handle my donations on my website, so when anyone inquires I send them to that webpage and then wait to hear from them. You may want to take the time to go by my website www.creationsbyelder.com and check it out for yourself.

Basically what I do is require them to make the request at least 30 days prior to the actual event. They have to give me the details of the event. In addition, if they have literature that has sponsorship mentions, I require that I am mentioned in that area along with my website URL to help drive traffic to it.

Also where the piece is displayed they have to show my name and my studios name. The amount they get from the piece is a "split commission" of 50% with a reserve amount set by myself and that the reserve amount is actually notated on the piece so donors know there is a minimum bid required.

Payment to me must be made within 7 to 14 days of the item being sold. They are responsible for any damages while the piece is in their care. If they are a 501c3 (non-profit organization) that I receive a tax letter for their part of the donation. Which I can use on my taxes at the end of the year.

This may sound like I am making them jump through a lot of hoops and I am. It substantially limits the amounts of actual requests I get each year for donations.

The reason I do this is to limit my loses and focus my efforts on those that really put forth the effort. Normally I am not donating just a little suncatcher in these instances. I am instead donating an item that is worth several hundred dollars or more.

I have in the past seen donations that I made that should of brought in several hundred dollars end up getting sold for less than a hundred dollars.

That ended up having very little positive effect for the charity and cost me time and money.

If I am going to donate a small suncatcher I just do it and not worry about making these folks jump through the hoops, but that is a rarity. I would rather do something substantial to help them out and if I am doing that I just can not afford to give it all away.

If you end up donating an item that has a reserve of $200 on it and say for instance it ends up selling for $300, the charity gets $150 to help them out and you get $150 to offset the cost of materials and the time spent to produce the item for them.

It is a win win for both parties.

As a side note I have a line of products that I developed where I give a portion of each sale to various charities. This is an ongoing effort on my part and spans a broad range of charitable concerns.

When you help out the community around you it is a good thing and when your customers know you actively do something for various charities it makes them feel good about spending money with you.

But at the end of the day it can not be to the detriment of your studio, that does no one any good.

Family

This is the sticky one. I know that I personally love to give items that I have made for birthdays and major holidays like Christmas to my friends and family. To me and I think also to the recipient, it just feels more special that way.

But you will inevitably be asked by a family member or friend to custom make something for them. It is not a matter of if that is going to happen but when it is going to happen.

This goes back to that "switch" that you flipped in deciding to turn this into a money making venture and you have to be in that mindset. You have to ask yourself "Is this going to cost me money?". I know that sounds very Scroogeish, but you have to start thinking like that.

Now I don't mean that you can't give them a good deal, what I am saying is just don't lose money in doing it.

Generally what I will do is quote them a price, like I do a customer. I tell them that this is what I would normally charge someone coming to me and ordering this item, but I am going to take off xx% for you.

In essence what I am going to end up pricing the item at is a level where it takes care of my cost of materials plus 50%. This takes care of waste and a little bit for my time.

Then I tell them I will work it in to my schedule while I am working on other client work.

If they have a set date they need the item by and say for instance there is little advance warning I may have to tell them that the discount is going to be much less because I am having to work longer hours for instance because I still have to keep my clients delivery dates.

Of course that is all up to you on how you handle these situations. The one thing I can tell you is that when you do something for free for someone, generally it holds little actual "value" to them. They may say how much it means to them and they fully mean what they are saying, but the real "value" is lost on them.

Chapter 11

Teaching

"Those that don't know must learn from those who do."
~Plato, The Republic

I have always enjoyed teaching and imparting knowledge to others that they find useful and broadens their horizons. For me, that moment you see a student literally "light up" with the understanding that they can actually achieve something they had thought they could not before, is priceless.

For those of you contemplating broadening your own horizons by starting to teach this wonderful art I would whole heartedly encourage you to do so. Without those of us with the knowledge and the willingness to pass on that knowledge, how can this art/craft/trade continue to thrive?

With that said I will also caution you to please be critical of your own abilities and limitations.

The reason I say this is that once you put on that teachers cap you are now setting the tone for how others in the future will perform and potentially how they too will in turn teach others.

So make sure you have good habits and good technical ability. In this day and age it is easy to find examples of proper technique and finished product on the internet, which means it is not hard to be able to compare your work to others, especially those that have been doing this type of work for awhile now.

The hardest thing you may do is judge yourself and your base of knowledge. You have to be honest with yourself, that is what you owe your future students.

Cross Training

This is a term we hear a lot in the professional world. Many of us have had jobs where we have heard that term used many times or used it ourselves. The same applies here.

One thing that I have noticed over the years is a decline in certain techniques being taught. A prime example of that is lead came work.

There can be numerous factors attributed to this decline but at the end of the day what has happened is we have fewer and fewer studios teaching that method and many that do teach it end up passing over it almost as if it is an after thought.

Sure, there are safety issues when working with lead. When handled properly and utilized with the proper safety methods employed there is negligible risk involved.

Now because of a lack of teaching the leading method you have a base of customers and hobbyists that only do copper foil work for instance. Then when they decide to start teaching what they know, they are limited to only teaching that one technique. We are loosing this knowledge slowly through attrition.

I give this as an example because I fully believe that when we know various techniques and we are teaching, we should teach those techniques.

A good beginners course will encompass a copper foil and lead project over a length of time that is sufficient to help the student acquire a solid understanding of the basics for each technique. So that they may then go home and perform those techniques with a degree of confidence.

When a student is not shown all those proper techniques it then makes the process of continued learning frustrating as well as the simple application of what they have learned. And when their frustration level increases they are more apt to decide to quit doing this type of work. It is very much a snowball effect.

I still teach classes, but on a one on one basis with a fairly intensive course in leading and copper foil. I also offer tele-presence help where I hone in on the exact area that someone needs help with and tutor them in that area.

I used to also teach numerous one day specialty classes which were very popular.

Classes on doing a specific suncatcher for a holiday, jewelry box, kaleidoscope, sand blast etching, acid etching, fusing, slumping, beadmaking etc... These were a one day Saturday class that would normally run from 9am to 4pm and gave the students good hands on knowledge of technique and normally were designed so that the pricing included them being able to take home a finished product.

In regards to pricing for various classes what I would suggest is that you do some comparison shopping online and with other studios in your vicinity. See how they do their classes and try to stay within those averages.

Keep in mind you have to provide value to your students and this is something new for you, you and your student are both going to be learning something new. You will be learning how to teach, they will be learning a new craft/art.

In Summary

As a general rule of thumb classes usually do not provide the bulk of your income and will not really start generating a decent amount of income until you are to the point of being able to sell supplies.

That is another consideration. If you are not going to be able to provide a steady and reliable source of materials for your students, are there other studios in the vicinity that will be able to? There is always the option for your students to order online, but when they first start out it is really nice for them to have that local resource.

I would suggest you wait until you have a retail establishment before pursuing teaching classes or do so in a highly specialized one on one setting. Make sure you are teaching them good habits and proper technique.

Chapter 12

Going Forward

Onward and upward is the only way to go!

If I were to try and give you advice for the future it would be do your best to learn more and more techniques and learn them properly. The more knowledge you have the better you will be able to perform services for your customer base. You will become more and more confident in your skills which in turn will make you more efficient over time as well.

One area I did not broach in this book is repair and restorations and the reason why is because that is a book by itself. I will be writing a book in the future in regards to repair and restoration services, the how, the why and basically the nuts and bolts of providing that kind of service.

The most important thing is to keep your passion. It is hard sometimes once you have flipped that switch and decided to make this your business and primary source of income.

There will be times you will not be able to work on projects you find "fun". But just keep in mind that the "boring" projects are helping pay your bills and allowing you to do the fun stuff somewhere down the road.

Just keep in mind how lucky you are to be doing something you love so much as your "job", not may people can say that.

Good luck to you and I wish you much success in the future.

Special Acknowledgement

I would like to take the time to say thank you to my wife Nita who has stayed with me through thick and thin and always encouraged me to follow my dreams. I look forward to our walker races.

I would also like to say thank you to Ethan, one of my sons, who has taken such a keen interest in this art. I hope that he continues forward and down this path as he has shown much aptitude. Just seeing his face light up when a customer comments on how much they love a piece that he has made is such a blessing to me.

I would like to thank the rest of my children for all of their encouragement over the years.

To my mother, Vivian, who passed away in 2012, thank you for being there for me and I know you are looking down with a big smile on your face. I love and miss you momma.

Printed in Great Britain
by Amazon